Amazing Bikes

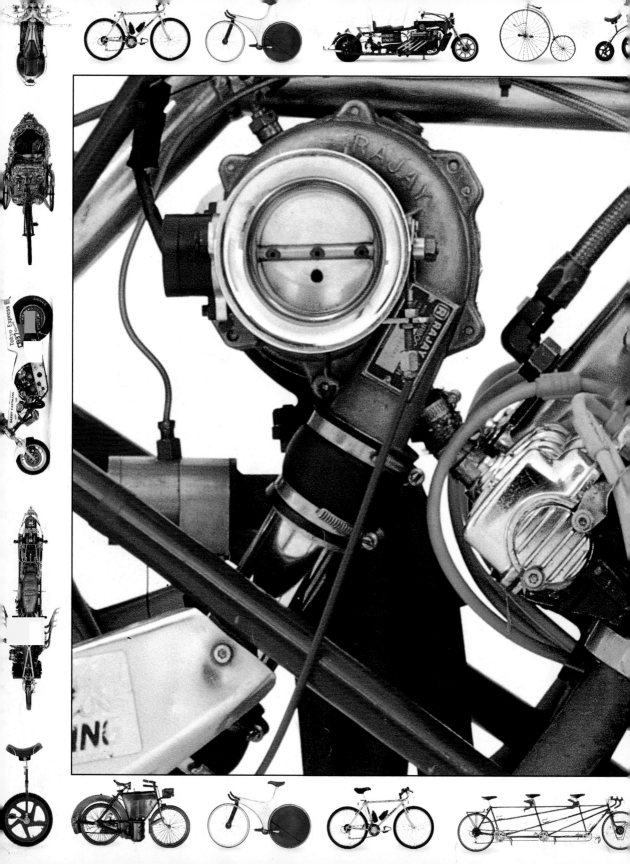

Amazing Bikes

WRITTEN BY
TREVOR LORD

PHOTOGRAPHED BY
PETER DOWNS

ALFRED A. KNOPF • NEW YORK

Conceived and produced by
Dorling Kindersley Limited

Project editor Louise Pritchard
Art editor Mark Regardsoe
Managing editor Sophie Mitchell
Managing art editor Miranda Kennedy
Production Shelagh Gibson

Illustrations by Bruce Hogarth and Julie Anderson
Bikes supplied by Bike UK (pp 26/27); Peter Burls (pp 20/21); Mike Burrows (pp 12/13);
Barry Eastman (pp 14/15); Mark Hall Cycle Museum, Harlow Council (pp 8/9, 18/19);
Museum of Mankind (pp 22/23); Les Nash (pp 24/25); Oddball Juggling Company (pp 28/29);
Science Museum (pp 10/11); Swallow Cycles, Essex (pp 16/17)
Special thanks to Streetbike Club; Dudley Hubbard for photography pp 22/23;
Adrian Whicher for photography pp 10/11; Phil Gatwood for photography pp 12/13;
David Fung and James Pickford for research

This is a Borzoi Book published by Alfred A. Knopf, Inc.
First American edition, 1992

Library of Congress Cataloging in Publication Data
Lord, Trevor.
Amazing bikes / written by Trevor Lord; photographed by Peter Downs.
p. cm. – (Eyewitness juniors; 22)
Includes index.
Summary: Highlights the history of bicycles and motorcycles, discussing unicycles
and other performing bikes, working bikes such as rickshaws, unusual bikes,
and bike racing.
1. Bicycles – History – Juvenile literature. 2. Motorcycles–
History – Juvenile literature. [1. Bicycles – History. 2. Motorcycles – History.]
I Downs, Peter, ill. II. Title. III. Series.
TL410.L67 1992 629.227'2–dc20 92-911
ISBN 0-679-82772-2
ISBN 0-679-92772-7 (lib. bdg.)

The author would like to dedicate this book to Louise

Color reproduction by Colourscan, Singapore
Printed and bound in Spain by Artes Gráficas Toledo, S.A.
D.L.TO:1297-1998

Contents

These children are about 4 ft tall. They will show you the size of the bikes in the main pictures

First bicycles

The first bicycles came in all shapes and sizes. Some of the early designs are still used today, but many, not surprisingly, were used only once.

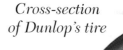
Cross-section of Dunlop's tire

Strips of sailcloth

Rubber coating

Air-filled inner tube

Riding on air

In 1888 John Dunlop was the first person to fit an air-filled tire to a bicycle. His idea changed the whole look of bicycles – not to mention their comfort and speed.

Swinging along

A swing bicycle was made in 1887. To make it go forward, the two riders pulled down on levers to swing the basket. This made the bicycle roll along.

Up and over

Mounting a high-wheeler takes practice. The rider puts one foot on the step, uses the other foot to scoot the bike forward, then stands up on the step and vaults onto the seat. Easy!

Cord attached to the brake. The brake is worked by winding this cord around the handlebars.

No knees

Most men wore jackets and knee-length trousers for cycling. Women wore trousers carefully designed so as not to show the knees.

Tires made of solid rubber

Coining a name

The high-wheeler was nicknamed the penny-farthing in Great Britain because its big and little wheels reminded people of two coins – the penny and the farthing. There were different kinds of high-wheelers. This one was made in 1871.

Footrest for use when speeding downhill

A long walk

Hobbyhorses were used in the early 1800s. They did not have pedals. The rider sat on the saddle and moved the bike by running along.

Boneshakers

The boneshaker of the late 1860s was an early bicycle with pedals. It had a metal frame and metal tires on wooden wheels. It was uncomfortable to ride – which is how it got its name.

First motorbikes

It is often forgotten that motorcycles have existed for as long as cars – over 100 years. They have improved since the early days!

Slipping and sliding

Muddy roads, poor tires, and a heavy engine mounted high on the frame made the early motorcycles slide sideways on their wheels.

Lazy cyclist

One man could not find an engine small enough to fit on his bicycle. So he mounted an engine on a trailer behind his bike, which pushed him along.

Container for coke

Mudguard holds 5 gallons of water

Boiler and firebox

Instant power

In the early 1900s, it was easy to turn a bicycle into a motorcycle. A wheel, along with an engine to drive it, could be bought and bolted to the side of the bicycle.

Hot seat

Gottlieb Daimler, one of the inventors of the car, made the first true motorbike in 1885 before he made a car. His son rode for 8 miles on it – in spite of the seat catching fire!

Room for two

Single-seat motorcycles were made more pleasant by adding a sidecar. The first sidecars were made of wicker and gave little protection to the passengers.

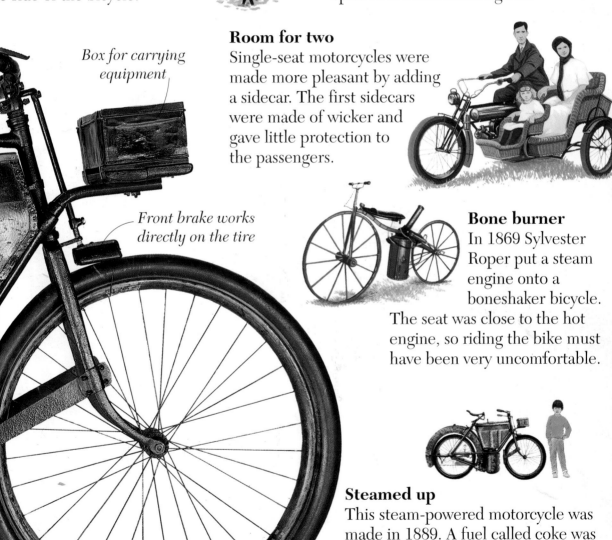

Box for carrying equipment

Front brake works directly on the tire

Bone burner

In 1869 Sylvester Roper put a steam engine onto a boneshaker bicycle. The seat was close to the hot engine, so riding the bike must have been very uncomfortable.

Steamed up

This steam-powered motorcycle was made in 1889. A fuel called coke was burned to heat water and make steam. The coke and water were kept in special containers within the cycle frame.

Bicycle sports

The first bicycle race took place in 1868. Today there are many kinds of bicycle races, and some unusual bicycle sports too.

Racing for glory
First run in 1903, the Tour de France race lasts 24 days and covers 2,500 miles. At the start of each day's racing the overall leader is given a yellow jersey to wear.

Pedaled ponies
In a game of polo, bicycles make good substitutes for ponies. Bicycles are cheaper, and the rider does not have so far to fall!

Brakes are operated by turning the right handlebar

Fast swordsmen
Cycling and fencing skills were needed in "ring-taking" races, which took place in Germany about 90 years ago. The cyclists raced around a track collecting rings on a sword.

Wheel fork has a blade on only one side of the wheel

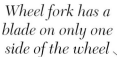

Cross riders
Mud, streams, grass, gravel tracks, and ditches are all tackled by cyclo-cross riders. Sometimes the muddy hills are so steep that the riders have to dismount and carry their bikes up.

Tough sport

A triathlon is a cycle race with a difference. The competitors swim, then cycle, and then run – without a break. Some races take over eight hours.

Built for speed

The modern racing bike below was designed by its rider for speed. It is the only one of its kind. It has no steel tubing, as ordinary bikes have, but a one-piece frame made of carbon fiber and filled with foam.

Help from the bank

Track racing takes place on oval tracks with steep sides, which the cyclists can use to help them go faster. The bikes have one gear and no brakes. The rider slows down or stops by pedaling slower.

Solid wheel cuts through the air better than a spoked wheel

Motorbike sports

Some motorcycle sports are fast, others are slow. Some take place in a stadium, others in the middle of a desert. All of them require skill and courage.

Keep it steady

Drag bikes race in twos on a track only ¼ mile long. The riders lean forward on their bikes to keep the front wheel on the ground. Bars are fixed on the back to keep the bike from spinning over backward.

Short burst

A drag bike starts and increases speed very quickly, reaching 200 miles per hour in seven seconds. At the end of a race the rider takes ½ mile to slow down and stop!

Fun in the sand

One of the hardest races the Paris (France)-Cape Town (South Africa) rally. The three-week race goes through the Sahara desert. In spite of the sand and the heat, riders reach speeds of over 100 miles per hour

BARRY EASTMA

1320   CBX

1,320-cc engine

3-inch-wide front tire with tread

Left only

Speedway riders race around a track. They always race counterclockwise, so the bikes only turn left. Just as well – they cannot go right as the kickstand would hit the ground!

Cool customers

Ice racing is a popular motorcycle sport in some countries. Long spikes are screwed into the tires so that they can grip the slippery ice.

Scraped knees

Motorcycle racers lean over so far on the corners that their knees touch the ground. The riders wear kneepads for protection.

On the rocks

The event known as "trials" tests the skills of balancing and handling a bike. Among other things, riders have to ride over rocks and tree trunks and are not allowed to put their feet down.

Rider has no seat

13-inch-wide back tire with no tread

Tokyo Express
CB37 *Racing*

MSD IGNITION

Display Signs [0895] 31762

Funny Bike 6

EAGLE

Out of the ordinary

Y ou will not see these machines on every street corner. They are custom-built, and some are even one of a kind.

Solar energy
People who get tired easily may like a bicycle like this. *Sunpower* has a solar-powered electric motor that can be turned on for extra power – especially useful when pedaling uphill!

Tire change
This bike can be pedaled on land and water. It can float on water with the wide tires, and for traveling on land it has tires with ordinary bike tires attached round them.

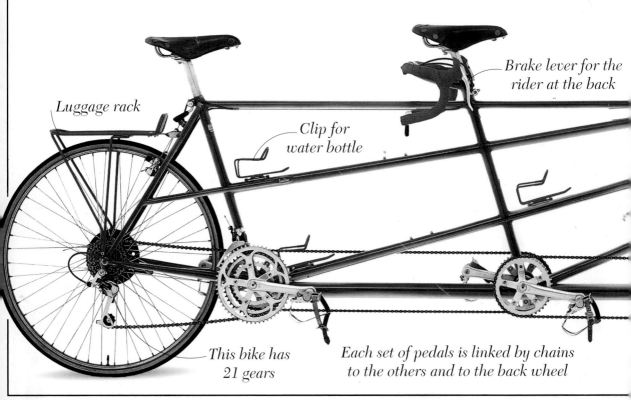

Luggage rack

Clip for water bottle

Brake lever for the rider at the back

This bike has 21 gears

Each set of pedals is linked by chains to the others and to the back wheel

Green bike

The Ecomobile has only two wheels but is enclosed in a body, like a car. It can go more than 160 miles per hour but uses less gas than a car – and takes up less room on the road too!

Made to measure

In the 1950s and 1960s people "chopped up" their bikes and added new parts to make "choppers." Choppers have long front wheel forks and high handlebars.

Balancing act

This "bike" was made in the early 1900s. It had a huge spinning wheel called a gyroscope (JIE-roe-scope) between the two passenger compartments. This worked like a spinning top to stop the vehicle from falling over when it was standing still.

Sharp corners

Bicycle wheels are always round, right? Wrong! Circus performers often ride bikes with square wheels!

Luggage holder

Bicycle built for three

Three British soldiers rode this triple-tandem bike 5,000 miles across the USA from New York City to Cupertino, California. Their eventful trip took 11 weeks.

Three-wheelers

B ikes that have three wheels are called tricycles. They are not made only for young children – tricycles have many different uses.

Sociable outing

Two people sitting side by side is a sociable, or friendly way to travel, and this kind of tricycle is known as a sociable. The different-sized wheels on this 1880s model are like those of the high-wheeler, or penny-farthing, perhaps it should have been called a two-penny farthing.

Terrific trike

In 1896 a giant tricycle was made in the USA. The two back wheels had a diameter of 11.5 ft, and it took eight people to pedal the machine.

Back wheels tilted toward each other

Handlebars

Rider lay back in the seat

Wheel chair

Tricycles help disabled people to get around. Some models are made to be "pedaled" by hand instead of by foot.

Car or bike?

With a chain, and the engine and back wheel of a motorbike, this Morgan three-wheeler is as much a motorcycle as it is a car. Said to have the speed of a motorcycle and the comfort of a car, it is known as a cyclecar.

Three-seater

A tricycle can be useful for shopping trips. This one has two seats for children and space underneath for the groceries.

Cyclops

Restricted view

Cyclops was built in 1986 to be the fastest human-powered vehicle, but it failed. It – and its rider – were enclosed in a fiberglass body. The rider used an eye doctor's instrument to see out – through a tiny hole in the front of the body.

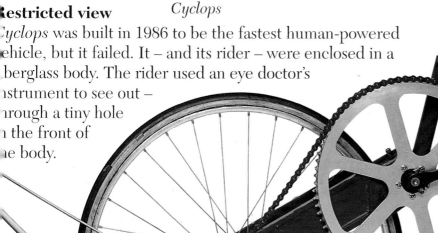

Attachment for cover

Pedal

Large chain wheel

Scooters

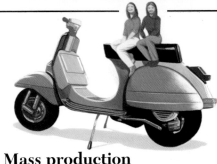

Scooters and mopeds are small, light, and cheap to run. Most of them cannot go as fast as motorbikes, but they are still great fun to ride.

Mass production

This extra-large Vespa scooter was built for publicity at a bike show. Vespas were first made in 1947 and are now the third most popular motor vehicles in the world.

From water to land

In 1952 Georges Monneret crossed the English Channel on a scooter. The scooter was mounted on floats, with a propeller driven by the back wheel. When Monneret landed in England, he removed the floats and rode the scooter to London.

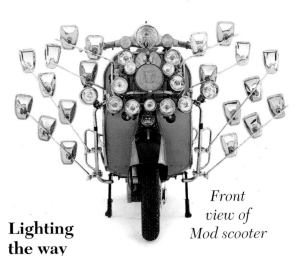

Front view of Mod scooter

Brake pedal

223·ARK

Lighting the way

If you were a "Mod" in Great Britain in the 1960s, you had to have a scooter. And the more lights and mirrors it had, the more fashionable it was. There are many fans of Mod scooters today. This scooter has 17 lights and 20 mirrors!

Dropped from the sky

In World War Two small scooters were folded up inside containers and dropped by parachute for some of the soldiers.

...tanding room only

...ome of the first scooters, ...ke this autoped of 1916, ...ere copies of a child's ...cooter – with an engine ...tached. Like the ...hildren's version, they ...ere ridden standing up.

Pedal power

In some countries you have to wear a helmet on a motorbike but not on a moped. In Florida the rider of an old Harley-Davidson motorbike persuaded a police officer that he didn't have to wear a helmet – his bike had pedals, so it was really a moped!

Seat for two people

Hook on which to ...ang helmet

Passenger footrest

On and off

A moped is like a bicycle with an engine. On this French moped the engine turns a roller, which is touching the front wheel. When the moped is standing still, the engine is lifted off the wheel.

Bikes at work

Bicycles and motorbikes are not ridden just for fun. Many have a tough working life.

Emergency!

In some cities emergency workers use motorbikes. They carry the same equipment as ambulances but can get to the scene of an accident sooner.

Message on a bike

As long ago as 1911, the British Post Office used motorcycles for delivering mail. This one is a Rover – a make which later became famous for its cars.

Sight for sore eyes

Some onion sellers in France cycle around with strings of onions on their handlebars. And to please tourists they often dress in traditional French costume.

Ice bike

Since 1922, tricycles have been used to sell ice cream. Some are still seen on hot days with their "cooler" on the front.

Street cleaner

This unusual bike is used in some cities to keep the streets clean. If a dog makes a mess, the "pooper scooter" comes and clears it away.

No problem

In some countries, people use bicycles more than cars. You can carry all sorts of things in the basket without tipping over.

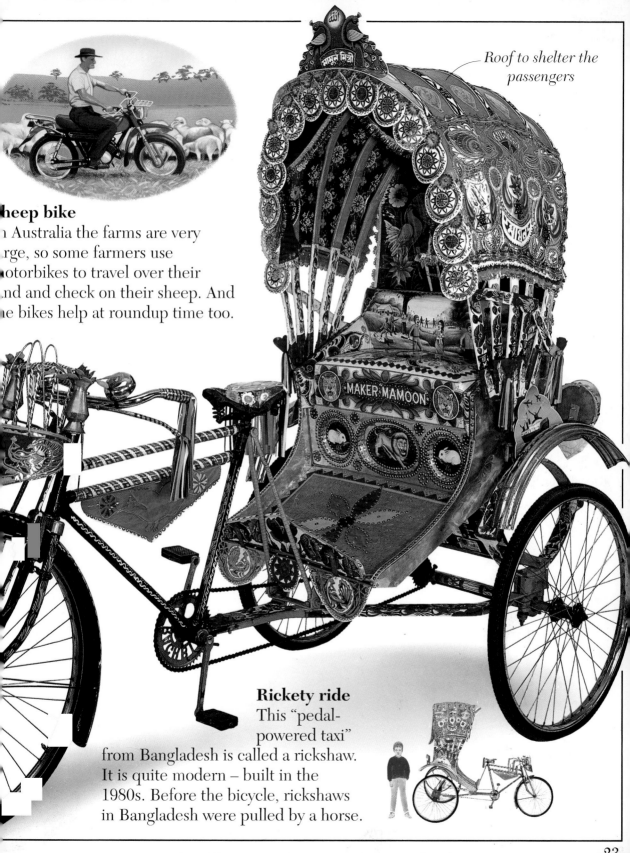

Sheep bike

In Australia the farms are very large, so some farmers use motorbikes to travel over their land and check on their sheep. And the bikes help at roundup time too.

Roof to shelter the passengers

MAKER MAMOON

Rickety ride

This "pedal-powered taxi" from Bangladesh is called a rickshaw. It is quite modern – built in the 1980s. Before the bicycle, rickshaws in Bangladesh were pulled by a horse.

For the record

The excitement of being the fastest or the longest, the slowest or the biggest, leads people to do some extraordinary things.

Flashed past

Donald Vesco set the motorcycle world speed record in 1978. His bike *Lightning Bolt* had two engines and reached a speed of over 318 miles per hour.

Bicycle built for 35

The bicycle with the most seats was made in Belgium. It is 66.9 feet long and carries 35 riders. The bike weighs more than 1 ton – over 60 times more than a normal bike.

Made it!

This is the longest motorcycle in the world – 12½ feet from the front tire to the end of the frame at the back (not including the towing hook). The bike was handmade in six weeks – for a bet!

Back wheel from a Jaguar car

Close call

John Howard pedaled his bicycle to an amazing record speed of 152 miles per hour. He managed this by riding close behind a car, which acted as a windshield.

Pyramid display

The Royal Signals Motorcycle Display Team of Great Britain set a record in 1986 when they formed a 36-person pyramid on eight bikes. They balanced long enough to travel 990 feet.

On one wheel

Doing a "wheelie" is riding a bike on just the back wheel. In 1984, Doug Domokos rode a 145-mile wheelie on his Honda. He stopped because he ran out of gas.

Engine from a Rover car

Front wheel and forks from a Harley-Davidson motorcycle

On your bike

We may have supersonic aircraft, high-speed trains, and fast, comfortable cars, but for some journeys, the best way to travel is still by bike.

Cycle for health
Cycling is good exercise. Many people who want to get fit use an exercise bicycle. It can be made easy or hard to pedal, and a meter shows how fast and how far you are pedaling.

Family fun
Bikes are made for people of all ages. Children's bikes and baby seats let whole families take to the road and enjoy themselves – sometimes all on the same bike.

Quick-release clamp for speedy adjustment of the height of the saddle

Modern design
Bicycle designs are always changing. New ideas to make bicycles go faster and ride more comfortably are being tried out all the time.

Out in the wilds
A mountain bike (right) can be ridden on almost any kind of ground, so a mountain bike rider can explore off the main roads.

21 gears

Off to work
Many people bicycle to work, as it is cheaper than going by bus or train. And on today's busy roads bicycling is often quicker than taking the car. Some towns and cities have special lanes for bicycles so that cyclists do not get hit by cars.

Safe, not sorry
Cycle training teaches young cyclists how to ride safely. There is a lot to learn, from bicycle control and repair to road signs and traffic laws.

Gear lever on the handlebars within easy reach

Water bottle

Tires with thick tread for traveling off-road

Watery grave
People in Amsterdam, Holland, dump their old bicycles in an unusual place – the canals. Two dredgers take 10,000 bicycles out of the canals every year. It takes them two years to clear all the canals, and then they have to start again!

Stunts and thrills

From circuses and fairgrounds to specially filmed stunts, bikes of all types are used to create exciting spectacles. Many of these stunts are very dangerous.

Circus trick
A unicycle, which has one wheel and no handlebars, is difficult to ride. Some circus performers ride unicycles while juggling or balancing things on their heads – a trick best left to the experts.

A choice of two
This unicycle can be changed into a two-wheeler for the most difficult acts.

Unicycle with two wheels

Missed the bus
Eddie Kid was only 16 when he jumped over 13 double-decker buses on his motorcycle in 1976. It was a world record.

An Evel job

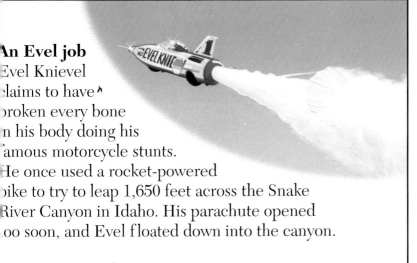

Evel Knievel claims to have broken every bone in his body doing his famous motorcycle stunts. He once used a rocket-powered bike to try to leap 1,650 feet across the Snake River Canyon in Idaho. His parachute opened too soon, and Evel floated down into the canyon.

Step by step

Many crazy stunts have been done on a bicycle. One of the craziest was cycling down the steps of the Eiffel Tower in Paris, France – all 1,710 of them!

Teamwork

Motorcycle display teams perform exciting and often dangerous routines. They have many practice sessions together so that every member of the team does exactly the right thing at the right time.

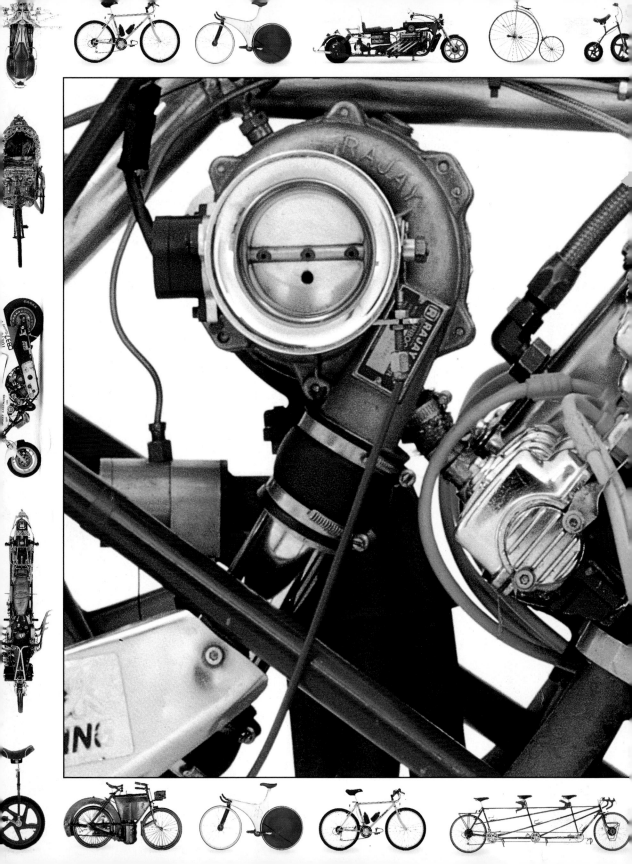